ANGER MANAGEMENT

How to Take Control of Your Anger, Develop Self Control, and Live a Happier Life

Table of Contents

Introduction

Do you regret doing certain things in your life? Do you regret having committed certain actions in the past? Do you feel like your life would have turned out differently if you only managed to handle yourself better at certain crucial times in your life? Do you hate it when you feel like you can't control your actions because you just get so heated?

If any of the above applies to you, chances are, you are struggling with emotional control. Chief among these, of course, is anger.

Believe it or not, anger is not all negative. I know, it's crazy, but a lot of people automatically think that if you are having anger issues, then this is an unqualified disaster. They think that nothing good could come out of it.

Well, it's not the all-consuming, all-burning emotional fire we're often taught to believe it is. In fact, we are conditioned to hold back, contain, or even deny our anger. Believe it or not, it can be positive and beneficial. However, for it to benefit us, we have to be able to control it properly. This is the key.

Unfortunately, this is also the reason why too many of us struggle with anger issues. We have a tough time controlling anger because we suffer from a bad definition of it and we are not prepared to exercise our will over it.

Even if we try to get ready for it, we often use the wrong techniques to deal with it and we fail again and again. Not surprisingly, anger continues to get the better of us and we end up making our lives worse through:

- ✓ Broken relationships
- ✓ Hurt or unaddressed feelings that linger
- ✓ Past emotional and psychological wounds that only fester as time goes by
- ✓ Emotional and mental habits that corrode our ability to control our lives

I've got some great news for you. Things don't have to continue like this. You can get the upper hand on anger.

This book teaches you how to deal with anger in a practical, adult and sustainable way. You will learn the following:

- ✓ Be clear about the situation
- ✓ Select what you're emotionally focusing on
- ✓ Understand what you're emotionally focused on
- ✓ Choose to resolve things positively
- ✓ Choose to channel your focus on learning
- ✓ Use 'defusion' steps

- ✓ Choose to read the situation under the best light possible
- ✓ Focus on the negative consequences if you act out in anger

Chapter 1: You Need to Control Your Emotions if You Wish to Live a Happy and Productive Life

I wish I could tell you that the only thing you need for success in life is a high IQ. It's very easy to see why many people believe that. After all, the ability to comprehend new information and apply it to daily situations is a highly prized trait. Not everybody can perform at high levels as far as this ability is concerned.

But unfortunately, there are a lot of people with otherwise high IQs who end up struggling. It's not because they don't know what to do. Instead, they do not know how to handle situations involving other people and their emotions. They may have everything that they need as far as intellectual processing and rational capabilities are concerned, but these don't serve them all that well when their emotions are involved.

Not surprisingly, in any organization, it's usually the people who are good at presenting ideas to other people and managing other people's egos and ambitions who rise to the top. These are not the sharpest tools in the shed. Not by a long shot.

In fact, in any typical organization, a lot of geniuses are in the technical department or some other areas while the top spots are taken by people who obviously do not have the highest IQs. Instead, they are emotionally intelligent. They know how to handle and channel their emotions in such a way as to maximize results. Make no mistake about it, you need that level of control if you want to live a happier and more productive life.

How Exactly Can Better Emotional Control Help You?

Just in case you're unclear as to why you need a better handle on your anger, here are just some of the ways better emotional control can benefit you:

Better Relationships

If you know how to watch what you say and how to better react to what people say and do around you, chances are, your relationships would improve. You would be more patient with people, and guess what? People would be more patient with you. There will be a lot more understanding and you would solve more problems together.

Also, you will be able to resolve potential conflict before they flare up into bigger problems. You would know how to get along better and the relationship improves over time.

Better Decisions

Being able to handle your emotions enables you to avoid making rash or impulsive decisions. When somebody says the wrong thing to you, it's very easy to feel wounded, threatened or even humiliated. Your natural tendency would be to push back emotionally. You may say something that would put the other person "in their place." You might even get so heated that you find it almost irresistible to ball up your fist and smack the other person.

Well, with better emotional control, you don't do those things. Instead, you are able to stick to your highest values and defuse what would otherwise be career-ending, relationship-destroying, and even law-breaking behaviors. You are able to keep what you want to really say and do locked within your mind. Instead, you say and do things that are more conducive.

Now, this doesn't mean that you don't want to beat the other person up. None of this means that you are immune to the tendency to give the other person a couple of slaps because whatever they said hurt you so much. But you decided to go with your better angels. It takes emotional control to take the high road, which is the better decision.

Better Crisis Management

Make no mistake about it, if you are a very emotional person, chances are, you will always end up making things worse for yourself and people who depend on you whenever a crisis happens. It's like pouring gasoline on charcoal. If you have all these anger and emotional control issues brewing or boiling deep within you, what would seem like a small, easily explained and very manageable crisis can flare up into an uncontrollable disaster. Everything turns into an emergency.

By choosing to deal with your anger issues appropriately, you would be able to get out from under the tendency to make crises worse than they already are. Instead, by focusing on rational, objective and mature decision-making, you may be able to control many crises in your life. Instead of constantly freaking out and running around like a chicken with its head cut off, you would be able to tackle situations in a calm, collected and mature manner.

This enables you to deal with issues with the proper perspective and, chances are, you would be able to handle whatever emergency breaks out in your life in a more positive way. You get burned less and there are less negative consequences. Sometimes, these might even lead to greater opportunities.

Better Perspective

In any kind of situation that involves conflict, it's easy to let our emotions get the better of us because we have an overblown and exaggerated perception of what just happened. Now, everybody's entitled to their feelings, but you have to understand that there is such a thing as reality.

Reality is made up of facts, and if you constantly assume too much, exaggerate, or even blow things out of proportion, don't be surprised if your perception of reality gets skewed. As a result, you end up reacting in the worst way possible to situations that would have otherwise been manageable.

Now, this doesn't mean that they're not negative. This doesn't mean that you're just going to fool yourself or deceive yourself into thinking that things are not what they are. No. You're still looking at the world based on reality. You're still focusing on facts. But instead of blowing things up out of proportion, you focus on how things are instead of what you wish they would be. This enables you to make more realistic decisions.

Now, this doesn't mean that these decisions are ideal. There are many situations in life where you just basically have to make do with the best choice, given the circumstances. Usually, these are far from ideal, but this is a better position than always opting for the worst decision possible. And unfortunately, if you let your emotions get the better of you, that usually happens.

Increased Self-Confidence

Believe it or not, if you are able to control emotions, your sense of trust in doing the right things at the right time to produce the right results increase quite a bit. Nothing's more damaging to Self-Confidence than the feeling that regardless of what you do, people just have it against you.

This is a very self-defeating mindset, but unfortunately, you do it to yourself. When you fly off the handle or say the worst thing to people because you're feeling threatened and you're angry, you end up in a downward spiral.

Do you think people are just going to take all of that sitting down? Do you think they're just going to say to themselves, "Well, this person is just the way he is and I'm just going to take this punishment from him."? No.

People are going to push back and you end up in a race to the bottom. People treat you worse. You then start wondering why people don't like you and, eventually, you become less confident in doing many things in many areas of your life.

Increased Self-Esteem

Self-esteem really is your opinion about your sense of worth. It's your opinion of whether you are likable enough or whether you are worthy of respect, love, affection, and admiration. If you are a very emotional person and you get angry a lot, it's very easy to internalize the conflict and defense mechanisms you provoke from other people.

If people hate being around you because you always fly off the handle and you say the most cutting and damaging things to them, you start absorbing all of these and sooner or later, you start feeling, "Maybe a bad person. Maybe I'm not worth knowing. Maybe there's something wrong with me. Maybe I am defective." And on and on it goes.

Unfortunately, just like the issue with Self-Confidence above, this is completely self-inflicted. With better emotional management, you don't have to go down that route. Your self-esteem improves because you are able to bring out the best in yourself and, ultimately, in other people.

This gives you a better perspective of your value as a person. It starts off with you feeling that you're not all that bad, and then it improves from that point forward.

You Get Greater Personal Peace, Calm and Serenity

The interesting thing about emotional control is that it gives you ownership of who you are deep down inside. It really does.

Because a lot of people who have problems with their emotions think that the problem comes from outside—it's other people saying the wrong things, it's them finding themselves in the wrong situation with the wrong input, it's everybody else's fault, not theirs. So, they spend a tremendous amount of time passing the blame to everybody else.

Also, they make all sorts of excuses. This leads to a very turbulent inner core. Since you're burning so much energy looking for the next group of people to blame for your failures or your inadequacies, there's all this inner conflict. It's very hard for you to just accept things. It's very hard for you to just sit back and relax.

With greater emotional control, you would understand that there are certain things in life that you really cannot control. You accept these, and you move on. That's right, you get over them. And by focusing on the things that you can control, this inner space of peace, calm and serenity continues to grow.

And interestingly enough, your sense of control grows with it. You're no longer feeling that whenever you go somewhere new or you deal with certain people, you just get thrown into this uncontrollable vortex of negative emotions, negative words, confrontation, and even negative actions. Instead, you bring your peace wherever you go because you start operating from this core inner area of peace, calm and serenity. This is possible with increased emotional control.

Less Internal Damage

As you can probably already imagine, just by reading the previous items I described above, reacting in the worst way possible to external stimuli leads to profound damage to your emotional, psychological, and physical health. These all flow together.

And when you are so conflicted, both internally and socially, don't be surprised if your immune system suffers. Don't be surprised if you're unable to sleep well. Don't be all that shocked when you become psychologically unstable. All that stress and pressure can come to a head.

Understand that you only need to control your emotions to make your life so much better on so many different levels.

I hope all of these benefits are clear to you because they are definitely worth working towards. Make no mistake about it, being unable to handle your emotions in a productive and positive way is not sustainable. Eventually, something's going to give. And unfortunately, the damage cuts across the board. We're talking about your relationships, your career, your ability to even function physically—all of these are impacted.

Chapter 2: 5 Common Myths About Anger

In this chapter, I'm going to walk you through 5 commonly held myths about anger. We need to cover this information because a lot of people hang on to these subconsciously. I'm telling you, if you believe these in any way, shape or form, at any level, you are not going to make any progress overcoming this emotion. Forget about it. It's just not going to happen. These tend to short circuit and override the information that I'm going to teach you in the following chapters.

You need to get your mind right about these common myths. Be aware of them and honestly assess whether you subscribe to them at some level or another. You may be thinking that you somewhat believe in them, and that it's really not all that bad—well, think again.

If you believe in these at any level, you are just making things unnecessarily harder on yourself. These work to trip you up and, ultimately, hold you back and drag you down so that any kind of emotional management technique is going to feel like you're pulling teeth. Who needs that extra stress?

Identify these myths in your life and work to completely debunk and forget about them.

Myth #1: Anger is always negative

When you were a kid, chances are, you engaged in some sort of tantrum. Chances are, you had some sort of emotional outburst and guess what happened? Your mom or your dad stepped in and told you were being a brat. Your anger is very bad and you should stop.

Now, when they repeat this enough time, you start changing your behavior. Externally, your parents do not see those outbursts. They feel good that you were making "progress." You probably got rewarded, either verbally, emotionally or in the form of a treat.

Unfortunately, just because you're not verbalizing your anger or "negative emotions," it doesn't mean that you made it go away. Instead, just like with most kids, you internalized it.

Think of it this way, you can explode a barrel of gasoline in a field outside and it can cause quite a bit of damage. There might be a crater created. There might be rocks and dirt thrown all over the place. Alternatively, you can take that gasoline and put it in a block of steel and detonate it. In other words, you can explode that gasoline in a combustion engine. This is how car engines work.

But, it's still an explosion. People don't see it from the outside, but that's what's going on. You don't see all these massive fires and explosions going around you when people turn the ignitions of their cars, but these explosions are going on nonetheless. Just because it's internalized, it doesn't mean that it doesn't exist.

This is what happens when you are given the impression by your parents that anger is always negative. So, you internalize this anger and it starts burning you up from within. You find it hard to forgive. You paint people in terms of black and white, either they're your friends or they're your enemies.

You feel that you're denying your emotions or you're being somehow contained, and this leads you to act out in other ways. This may be more socially acceptable, but you're still acting out. You're still channeling all that energy, and there's a tremendous amount of negativity behind it.

Myth #2: Anger is triggered by other people or external situations

According to this thinking, anger is caused by other people. It's caused by what other people say, what they do, or other stimuli that comes in from the outside world. Basically, you have to see something, hear it, smell, taste, or feel it for anger to just well up in you. Well, what if I told you that it's the other way around?

I know it sounds crazy, but unfortunately, when people think that anger is external in nature, they fall into the trap of thinking that they only need to hang out with the right people. They only need to find themselves in "optimal" situations and they will kiss their anger or emotional control issues goodbye.

This is going to be a serious problem because you're going to be walking on eggshells. You're going to be making all sorts of compromises and getting into all sorts of artificial situations in your life trying to run away from your emotional issues.

It's actually not what's outside of you that is the problem. Because let's face it, external stimuli are essentially neutral. It's your interpretation of these stimuli that determines whether you're angry, sad, happy, hopeful, shocked and a whole range of other emotions.

Unfortunately, this myth of external stimuli being the ultimate cause of emotions is all too common. So, people then bend over backward and really warp their lives trying to avoid triggering such situations.

I'm sorry to be the one to tell you this, but it doesn't matter how far you run away from these, it's always going to get you because your anger stays with you. How come? Well, it's not your external situations that trigger anger and "bad emotions." It's your internal reading of your external world that is to blame.

Myth #3: Anger is a show of aggression and signals dominance

A lot of guys subscribe to this myth. They think that anger is essentially perfectly acceptable because it really boils down to social hierarchy. You have to express anger to essentially call people out and communicate your position in any kind of social hierarchy you find yourself in any situation.

The problem with this thinking is that it causes unnecessary conflicts. It tricks people into thinking that anger is the optimal dominance signal. It blinds people to the fact that there are other ways to show dominance and hierarchy.

You don't necessarily have to compete and crush other people. Anger can burn, it can cut, it can crush. You can still demonstrate where you are in the hierarchy of things without necessarily stepping on other people.

Sadly, a lot of people, especially men, believe in this. Of course, the older the guy is, the more of a clue they would have so they tend to step away from this. But when it comes to younger guys, this can be a serious problem.

A lot of younger guys have something to prove, and in their minds, there's nothing simpler than using anger as a dominance signal. This, of course, leads to a lot of conflicts because there are many other young guys who think the same thing. So, you have a lot of people bumping heads, not just figuratively, also literally.

Myth #4: Anger highlights taking control

A lot of people believe that when you're angry, you are just focused on the moment and you're taking control of the situation. While there is a lot of truth to this because anger can be a mental state of extreme clarity, you're paying a high price for it.

It's kind of like trying to light up an interior space in your home by dragging in a barrel and lighting gasoline inside the barrel. It does the job, sure. There's a lot of light created. You're able to see a lot of previously dark areas. The problem is, there's a strong chance that you'll burn down your home. Wouldn't an LED flashlight do a similar job without the fire risk?

Unfortunately, a lot of people think this way. They think that the only way they feel that they're actually taking control of certain issues in their life is when they feel a tremendous amount of anger. They think that it is the most obvious way to detect points of emotional clarity.

Well, you're paying too high of a price. That's like burning down your house just to get rid of a few rats. There are less destructive approaches. Again, anger is not always negative, but if handled improperly, it creates more problems than it solves.

Myth #5: Anger is always cathartic

Hey, I'm a big catharsis fan. All of us, at some level or another, need to get stuff out of our system, and that sense of release when all that negativity, all those unaddressed issues and those aches and pains just flow out can be the most liberating feeling.

Now, with that said, there are many ways to experience catharsis. While being angry can lead to that outpouring of emotion, just as I have mentioned in the discussion with Myth #4, you may be paying a high price. Sure, you're getting stuff off your chest and you're unclogging a lot of your emotional pathways, but you may be burning a lot of bridges at the same time. You may be saying things that cut and crush so deeply that they come back to haunt you.

You have to understand that one of the top reactions people feel when they get hurt is to get back. It's perfectly natural. It's part of the human condition. You want revenge. You want payback. So sure, anger can be cathartic, but there are other emotions that produce the sense of release.

Don't, for a moment, believe that anger is always cathartic. Don't believe that this is the only path to emotional release.

Also, a lot of people get really angry and they fail to get that release. I mean, talk about a lose-lose situation. It's bad enough that you put your emotions on center stage and a lot of people are at risk of getting burned, that's disastrous enough as it is. But despite all of that, you still did not get stuff off your chest.

Instead, you just burned a lot of people, you emitted a lot of heat, but there's very little light as far as you are concerned. The unresolved issues still remain unresolved. The emotions that are fueling the anger, they still remain untapped.

This is the danger that you run if you believe that anger is always cathartic. Regardless of how many times you do it, if you don't do it right, the deep problem still remain while you're creating a whole host of new problems for yourself.

You need to get out from under these common myths. I need you to take a step back and think, seriously, about these myths. Do you believe them at any level? Do you somewhat believe them? Do you believe them completely? Do many of your assumptions contain these beliefs?

You have to ask yourself these hard questions. You have to probe deep. Don't leave any emotional or psychological stone unturned.

If you, in any way, believe these myths, you are going to trip yourself up as you try to get out from under your anger issues. It's not a question of if, but when. That's how negative these myths are. They will give you all sorts of reasons to stop making progress toward better emotional health.

You have to understand that human beings are creatures of habit. We've grown accustomed to doing things and feeling about things a certain way. While we may understand and welcome the benefits outlined in Chapter 1, deep down inside, we want the status quo. We may be miserable, but it's the misery that we are used to.

Always remember this. This is why you need to crush the myths above because ultimately, your own mind is going to start working against you and it only needs to tap into these myths for you to start backsliding. Whatever progress you made starts eroding.

Chapter 3: The Reality of Anger

Now that I've stepped you through the myths and misconceptions surrounding the emotion of anger, let's get real. Let's focus on what the reality is. By focusing on how things are, you will do a better job changing your relationship with anger. You would be in a better position to handle this otherwise explosive emotion.

No myth in the world, no wishful thinking or misconception is going to help you achieve much progress. You may be able to deal better, at least superficially, but deep down inside, things are still unresolved, and don't be surprised if they bubble up to the surface. In fact, don't be all that shocked when you experience an explosion because you hung onto those myths and misconceptions.

Focus instead on the reality of anger. Base your strategies on these. Build them on something real.

Reality #1: Properly Channeled, Anger Can Produce Positive Results

You have to remember that anger is just an emotion. That's what it is. You don't have to let it get the best of you. Instead, you can channel it. You can use it the right way.

We have anger for a reason. This can be a properly valid emotion in the right context. Handled properly, it can make situations better. If anything, anger gives you emotional urgency.

It doesn't mean that you have to express it in the worst way possible and damage your relationships. It doesn't mean that just because you feel this tremendous intensity that you have to project it out to other people and burn them as well. Instead, you can use this urgency of living in the moment to focus on the right things so you can do the right things at the right time to produce the right results with the right people.

The best part to all of this is that regardless of what's going on around you, you can focus on what's true about anger. And to get that emotional urgency, you need to take action.

You have to understand that a lot of people struggle in life because they don't let things reach that level. They know what they should be doing, they know that there are many things in their lives that they are not exactly happy with, but there is a big divide between knowing what to do and knowing why you should do it, and actually taking action.

You need a sense of urgency to push you off the fence. Constantly kicking around things that you believe you should be doing is not going to do you much good. The more you think about these things and the more you refuse to take action, the more your life continues as before. Nothing changes. You might be thinking that you're getting wiser and wiser, but that doesn't really help you.

You have to understand that the world judges you based on what you do. It couldn't care less about what you're thinking. You can have all the best intentions and motivations in the world, but that's not going to do you much good. People only sit up and pay attention when you actually do things.

Please understand how this works because the anger that you feel might be that connection that you need to turn your realization of the things that you should be doing into actual behavior. Because once you start taking action, that's when your world starts to change because the world can't help but sit up and pay attention. Things get real when you take action. And properly channeled, anger can get you there.

Reality #2: Anger Comes from Internal Judgment and Analysis of Situations and Stimuli

What if I told you that everything that's going on around you is neutral? It may seem like an emergency, it may seem like it's the worst thing in the world, but really, it's neutral. What gives it meaning is the meaning you choose to impose on it.

You're constantly analyzing the stimuli you are picking up from the world based on your sense of sight, hearing, smell, taste, and touch. This raw data comes in and you give it meaning.

Instead of thinking that anger comes from some place outside of you, focus on the fact that it's your meaning of certain stimuli that makes you angry. Other people can choose to interpret this reality feedback in a different way and end up in a different emotional state. It really all boils down to the filter you choose to use. Don't get it twisted. Don't get it confused.

Even if you hang around with the seemingly most disagreeable people, you don't have to get angry. You don't have to get upset. It all depends on how you interpret what you perceive from the outside world.

A lot of people think that anger is episodic; that it's based on certain people doing certain things in certain situations. According to this thinking, you just avoid all of those factors and you should be good to go. Absolutely wrong. You end up running away from a lot of things in your life, your comfort zone starts shrinking, and at the end of that day, you're back to where you began.

Instead of running away from external triggers, focus instead on the filter you choose to use. Remember, you don't have to be angry. You don't have to go off on the deep end. It doesn't have to consume you. It's okay to be angry in a positive way. It's okay to have emotional clarity, but to take it to another level where it can get really negative is entirely your choice.

Believe it or not, this has little to do with what exists outside of you. Instead, it has everything to do with how you choose certain situations to be. Stop perceiving things a certain way and you'd be surprised at your reaction.

Reality #3: Anger Can Be Self-Directed, Aimless and Not Necessarily Aggressive

A lot of people think that anger is always explosive. A lot of people think that it only takes one direction: from inside to outside. No. It can actually be self-directed.

A lot of people who struggle with anger are actually angry at themselves. This eats them up. It burns them up from within. They put a tremendous amount of pressure on themselves. A lot of people actually commit suicide because of the stress.

Also, anger can be aimless. It's not like you're angry at one person, but you're just angry in general. So, it pushes you to emotionally walk around in circles. It's not focused, it's not directed, it's purposeless.

Instead, it's just this free-floating anger that's basically your default reaction. Accordingly, you basically chase your own tail, emotionally speaking.

Reality #4: Anger Often Flows from a Sense of Lack of Control

When people feel angry, a lot of the times this is due to the fact that they feel that they're really not in control of the situation. They feel really frustrated and they essentially just throw a tantrum.

They lash out. They say really damaging things, not just to other people, but to themselves. It's just this raw emotional outpouring and it often traces back to a sense that you really are not in control of the situation.

Now, this is rich because, as I've mentioned above, you are always in control of how you analyze or respond to a situation. To one person, a fire or a robbery may seem like the end of the world, but to another person, it's a solvable problem. I mean, in their mind, it's not ideal, but people can get over them. And it really boils down to what kind of mindset or mental filter you select.

Unfortunately, when you choose to get angry, it really boils down to the fact that you've sensed that you don't have control over the situation. The problem here is that you're trying to control the situation instead of controlling your response to the situation. These are two totally different things with two totally different results. They lead to different paths.

Understand how this works because if you always feel that you have to control everything that's going on in your life, you're going to run yourself ragged emotionally, physically, and spiritually. At the end of the day, don't be surprised if you have very little to show for all that time, effort and energy.

You might want to focus on the things that you can actually control. And unfortunately, this is actually very limited. And that's okay.

If you were to set up all sorts of unrealistic expectations for yourself and you let your idea of control track this really wide circle, don't be surprised when things fall apart. Don't be surprised when things fall through the cracks and you feel that you're not really in control. You need to use a different mental filter.

Reality #5: Anger Can Be Implosive in Nature Instead of Cathartic and Explosive

As I've mentioned in Myth #5, a very common idea about anger is that it's always cathartic; that people are just basically letting loose and this explosive outward direction of emotion clears a lot of emotional and mental cobwebs. If only that were the reality.

Often times, anger can take the opposite direction. Instead of exploding, you implode. Instead of projecting outwards, anger can involve some sort of internal vacuum, kind of like a black hole pulling in cosmic dust, debris, complete planets, solar systems, even galaxies.

This is one reality about anger that a lot of people are clueless about and it continues to harm them. They think that the problem is when they are projecting intense emotions in a negative way to other people around them. In their minds, as long as they're not doing this, then it's okay.

Well, you can beat yourself up. You can sell yourself short too often that your sense of worth and self-esteem suffer profoundly. What happens then? You end up crushing yourself. You end up defining yourself in such a way that you are a shell of who you could actually be.

Make no mistake about it, most people have what it takes to be extremely wealthy, powerful, and effective. But most of us live anonymous, desperate lives, making do with a fraction of the results that we are otherwise capable of producing. What's wrong with this picture? Where's the disconnect coming from? Well, a lot of it has to do with Reality #5.

Oftentimes, we are our worst critic, and we don't know why. Oftentimes, we have this intense emotional vacuum that nothing is good enough. This is just anger working the other way. It's imploding your ego. You're beating yourself up unnecessarily.

Now, don't get me wrong, there's nothing wrong with self-correction and self-criticism. Those are part of maturity. But you can take things to the other extreme. You can overdo things. And this produces all sorts of problems. And the worst part is that you're the last person to know.

Make sure that you have a clear idea of all the realities outlined above. They present all the factors that you need to deal with so you can manage anger in an effective way. Ignore these realities at your peril. If you continue to pretend that they don't exist or they don't apply to you, then don't be surprised if your anger remains.

You may be able to achieve lots of success by containing your anger, redirecting it in the best way you can, but eventually, you will hit a wall. Eventually, you will hit its limits because unless and until you base your anger management strategies on reality, nothing's going to change. You will just end up suppressing things until a later date until they bubble up again, or worse yet, explode to the surface.

Chapter 4: Anger and Your Personal Roller Coaster

Have you ever thought about somebody that did something really bad to you? Maybe they embarrassed you in front of a lot of people, maybe they punched you or made you feel small, or maybe they beat you and you really haven't gotten around to forgiving them.

Maybe a mental image of a past lover flashes into your mind and the only thing you can think about is how that person hurt you, made you feel small or betrayed you. Maybe the image of a boss comes to mind and you feel that you were trapped in that job and that you did not get appreciated. You did not get the promotions you felt you deserved. What happens when these things take place?

Usually, when the mental image flashes, you feel a tremendously negative surge of emotions. And depending on who you're with and where you are, sometimes you say certain things. In fact, in certain situations, you might even do certain things. Now, usually, these are not the things you would say or do, but these memories or triggers just bring out the worst in you.

Similarly, you may be with other people and then somebody says something and it triggers either a negative association with the past or you just react to it in the worst way possible. Instead of blowing it off or asking questions to create a context, you just blow up.

Of course, later on, you try to make all sorts of excuses why you reacted this way. Maybe the other person "had it coming to them," maybe you didn't want to look weak—whatever the reason may be, you know that you're just making up all sorts of "seemingly logical" justifications for why you did something wrong. Ideally, you would not have handled things that way. Welcome to your personal emotional roller coaster.

What if I told you that you are always on an emotional roller coaster? You probably would laugh. You probably would say, "Well, I'm a pretty logical person. I usually manage my emotions. How can you say I'm on a personal roller coaster?" Well, it really all boils down to the fact that you are your own reality editor. Seriously.

A lot of people are under the impression that reality is this objective set of facts that all people from all over the world will respond and process the same way. Man, if things were only that simple. Unfortunately, that's not reality.

You see, everything that you perceive, whether through your sense of sight, smell, hearing, touch or taste, are essentially neutral. What gives them meaning and which provokes certain reactions from you is your interpretation or analysis of them.

Think of the worst thing you can ever see. Well, that's actually neutral because it doesn't have to be the worst. It all depends on how you choose to look at it.

You're always in control of your ability to respond to these stimuli. In fact, I would go the extra step and say that you are constantly editing your reality. Here's how it works.

Step #1: Perceive Stimuli

Whether we're talking about your sense of taste, sight, smell, touch or hearing, you pick up signals from the outside world. This is very basic. Most people could agree on this. Either you hear something or you don't. Either you see it or you don't. It's perception—all these stimuli just coming in.

And, interestingly enough, it is neutral because a cup in front of me that says, "The Coffee Bean and Tea Leaf" is the same to people who can read English. It doesn't matter where they're from, it doesn't matter what they've seen in their lives, it doesn't matter how far they went in their educational pursuits, it's the same. It's a purple cup, with a purple heat jacket, a plastic cap, with a logo and the words "The Coffee Bean and Tea Leaf" right on the cup. It's neutral.

Step #2: Interpret Stimuli

The next step of the reality editing process is the meat and potatoes of your personal reality. While that cup of Coffee Bean and Tea Leaf will be seen by people from all over the world the same way, your interpretation can determine whether your experience is negative or positive.

Now, I'm looking at this cup and it doesn't really mean much to me because it contains the black coffee that I love to drink. Pretty straightforward, no big mystery, nothing to unravel, right?

Well, what if you and your ex-girlfriend broke up at a Coffee Bean and Tea Leaf because she told you she was in love with your brother or your best friend? And during that time, she was drinking from a cup that looks just like the cup that I just described above. That cup is going to mean something very different for you.

Similarly, if your boss likes to drink that brand of coffee and every time he calls you into his office to call you a worthless, no-good idiot, he drinks from that cup. What kind of interpretation do you think you would have the next time you come across a cup that looks like your boss's favorite cup of coffee?

These are extreme examples, but I hope you get my point. Your interpretation of stimuli is completely dependent on you. You choose that interpretation.

This interpretation works with an association. You associate an object that you see, touch, smell, taste and hear with certain situations and certain judgments.

Be aware that this is going on because ultimately, the item or the person or the words or the situation you are perceiving really has no meaning, in and of themselves. They're just stimuli. You're the one who is always in charge putting meaning into things.

And unfortunately, if you are having a tough time with anger, it's because you do not take ownership of this interpretation process. You choose not to be aware that you're editing your reality and, more importantly, you choose not to be clear about the interpretation that's going on and how it leads to emotional responses.

Now, I wish I could tell you that this only leads to some sort of emotional flare-up. It doesn't. See Step #4.

Step #3: Enter an Emotional State

The next step in the reality editing process is you entering an emotional state. Now that you have perceived a stimulus and you have analyzed it or put meaning on it, you enter an emotional state.

So, taking the coffee cup example, when you see that, it reminds you of your boss who used to insult you, degrade you, and of course, refuse to promote or give you a raise. Do you think you'll feel good? Well, unfortunately, since you focused on that association, the sight of that item won't make you feel good.

In fact, your blood pressure might rise and it starts to trigger all sorts of negative memories of that person. Maybe that person laughed at you when you came into work on crutches and said, "You're lame. Literally and figuratively." You might even think of all sorts of verbal abuse your boss heaped on you.

In that situation, it's very hard for you to step back because now you're in an emotional roller coaster. Once you have looked at the stimuli and it reminds you of that association, you're sucked into this emotional vortex. You start thinking of revenge fantasies.

You start thinking back on how your boss made you feel so small, humiliated and worthless. You start thinking to yourself of how powerless you are now and the kind of low-level jobs you have because of that one mean man that basically ruined your life—and to think that this was all triggered by a purple cup with a white plastic cap.

This emotional state is very real because your breathing pattern changes, your blood is definitely pumping, and all these mental images flash in your mind. By flash, I mean literally flash. All these thick layers of memories just zoom through your mind really quickly. I mean, that's how powerful your mind is. And they, in turn, trigger an emotional cascade.

You really can't quite put your finger on your emotional state because that's how many reactions are going on. On the one end, you're feeling angry, on the other end, you're feeling like you've wasted many years of your life so you feel foolish, on the other end, you feel frustrated about how your life has turned out and that there's a lot of regrets, and on and on it goes. You're in this emotional state.

Step #4: You Take Action

Now that you are heated, angry, upset and frustrated, don't be surprised if you take action. Now, please note the word "action." It doesn't necessarily involve balling up your fist and smacking somebody with it. It can also be you saying things in anger and frustration.

Your new boss might come in with a Coffee Bean and Tea Leaf cup and all of a sudden be the target of this raw unstated anger on your part. You're not saying anything yet, but all these negative thoughts are coming in. In fact, they may wash over you so much that you say something harsh to your boss. That's how you took action. It's completely verbal, but the emotions changed your behavior.

Always remember that taking action doesn't necessarily have to involve physical action. It can be verbal as well.

Step #5: Repeat the Process or Unwind It

Now, please understand that when you get into that emotional roller coaster, it's very hard to stop. It can be a self-reinforcing situation. Believe it or not, you do this because there's a reward.

When you look at that cup and it triggers that horrible boss you had that denied you, crushed your hopes, insulted you and demeaned you, you get a cathartic release. It feels good. In fact, don't be surprised if you've gotten addicted to that release.

So, it doesn't really take much for that association to be triggered. Either you see a cup, you can think of certain phrases that your boss used to like, or any other thing that reminds you of him. Whatever the case may be, you end up with a habitual action.

Now, again, this action can be mental, verbal or physical or any combination of the three. When you take this action, and there's the payoff, you get this release. And on and on it goes.

Thankfully, there is an alternative. You can continue to repeat the process or you can choose to intentionally unwind it.

Our Reality Editor Creates a Spiral

I hope my description above of the process has made it clear to you that there are actually two directions this can go. When you edit your reality, you can create an upward spiral. I know, it's hard to believe, but you can.

How? Well, when you perceive something, like when somebody smiles at you, you feel good. You feel appreciated. You feel like you matter, so you smile back at them and you say, "How are you doing? How have you been? Great to see you."

And then they bounce back that positive vibration to you, and they say, "I'm doing fine. How are you doing? Thank you for asking." And both of you feel more comfortable. Both of you feel good. That creates an upward spiral.

The more comfortable you get with each other, the more information flows, you love each other's company, and the personal bond grows. The flow of positive emotions grows. This is the upward spiral of the reality editing process.

Unfortunately, it also works the other way. You wouldn't be reading this book if the only spiral created by your social interactions is upwards. In fact, I would venture to guess that the reason why you're reading this book is that most of the time you are stuck with a downward spiral.

You feel really lousy because you're angry about something in the past, so when you see a barista at a coffee shop, you could barely smile. Instead, you scowl at that person. Now, that person has his or her own set of problems. Everybody's got their own. So, they do not treat you as well as they should, or you feel this way.

So, you feel bad, they feel bad, and you scowl at them even more. Don't be surprised if you don't get the kind of warm, all-encompassing emotional response. So, you feel even worse and you send off even more threatening or angry signals. And on and on it goes. It's a downward spiral.

But the good news here is that we're always in control of this process. Believe it or not, you have a direct role to play on whether you create an upward spiral or a downward one. You are always in control and it really boils down to how you interpret stimuli.

This really is the only place you can take control over because once you get into an emotional state, it's like trying to stop a freight train that has hit a very high rate of speed. Good luck. It's going to take a long distance for this train to slow down. Throughout all that time, the engineer of the train is basically pulling on that brake going crazy.

You have to exercise your will on your personal roller coaster at the stimuli interpretation part. In other words, you need to be mindful of the mental filter you're using.

If you consistently find yourself angry, upset, or your emotions get the better of you, you might want to change your filter. You might want to change your mindset. You might want to change the way you habitually analyze and interpret what would otherwise be neutral stimuli.

Master this Reality Editing Process

By changing your mental filter, you can read stimuli in an empowering way. Instead of instinctively or automatically reading things in the worst way possible, which leads to a lose-lose situation and negative emotional states, try to read the situation in a more empowering way.

Now, I'm not saying that this is easy. Nobody can make that claim. It's going to take some time. This is not going to happen overnight. But you really have no choice. You have to read the stimuli that you perceive in an empowering way. Make sure that they lead to the right emotions, which in turn leads to more positive actions.

Now, what makes this really difficult is that you're operating on many different levels here. You can't really change the stimuli. That's just going to happen. Living in this world, you don't know what kind of signals you will get. That's the world we live in. It's random. But the good news is that, ultimately, they are neutral.

What you can change is the stage where you're judging and analyzing things. This then leads to the right emotions.

Exercising better control at the analysis part leads to you controlling your emotions, which leads to the next level, which involves your actions. Whether you're saying stuff or actually engaging in the behavior, you exercise a lot more power there if you put a lot of time, effort and focus on reading stimuli in an empowering way.

The following chapters will touch on these and unpack them. But this is the core of the materials I'm going to teach you. Get this right and you will be living a more productive life. Continue to do what you're doing, and don't be all that shocked when you start imploding from within. It's your choice.

Chapter 5: Anger can Become an Emotional Habit

I hope you got the idea from my description of upward and downward spirals that anger can become habitual. Seriously. Pay attention to what I said about the release.

Well, that sense of release can get so exhilarating that you might actually seek out emotional downward spirals because you're looking for that reward. Again, this makes as much sense as burning down your house to get rid of a few mice, but this is exactly the kind of thing people engage in all the time.

You may be so angry at that boss of yours who you may fairly or unfairly blame for a lot of things that went wrong in your life that you are looking for situations to rehash this feeling to get that release going. It's like your way of getting back at him.

This can get really addictive because you focus on the reward so you engage in the negative interpretation again and again. And what makes this really ironic is that you gain a sense of control. In fact, this may be one of the emotional rewards that you get. You get to feel that "I can control this sense of revenge; this sense of taking action on my boss."

Well, you're basically just shadowboxing with the memory of your boss. For all we know, you may be shadowboxing with a cartoon. He or she may not actually be like that. You might actually be overlooking certain facts. You might actually be conveniently remembering certain things and conveniently forgetting others.

Whatever the case may be, this whole process gives you a sense of control because, at the back of your mind, you're thinking that you're taking action. The sense of humiliation, the perception of hurt, and all these negative interpretations are all too real in your mind. Not surprisingly, it feels good to "take action," at least mentally, by engaging in this downward spiral.

The Sad Reality

Well, what I just described above is how a lot of people think about their anger cycle. At some level or another, they feel that they're in control. This intensity makes them feel alive. It also gives them a false sense of taking action.

In reality, you're rehashing old drama and you are basically shadowboxing with something that may or may not exist. But what is real is that you are stabbing yourself again and again. Who's getting hurt? Who's being put at a disadvantage? Who's being left behind emotionally?

Let me tell you, it's not your ex-girlfriend. I'm definitely not your ex-boss. It's you because you became addicted to the negative emotional state. Sure, it may be cathartic, but at what cost? It's like stabbing yourself over and over again because you got this rush of endorphins, but little do you know that you may have stabbed an artery and you're slowly dying.

Understand What is Really Going On

That image of your boss is not really him or her. That scene with your girlfriend in your mind, that's not the reality. Instead, what's really going on here is that you're shadowboxing with your emotions. You're engaged in some sort of puppet show with your emotional states. You're not really dealing with the issue directly.

And this is part of the perverse rewards you get. You get that sense of control. You get that sense of taking action, without really taking action and really taking control. Do you see how this works?

It's kind of like trying to resolve a project that you know needs to get done, but instead of rolling up your sleeves, putting your nose to the grindstone and actually doing something, you worry about it. I'm telling you, that makes just as much sense as trying to change the weather by chewing gum. They are not in any way, shape or form connected.

You have to deal with the issue directly. Unfortunately, doing things this way just entrenches your emotional habits. It makes the false reward so much more intense that it makes it easier for you to crave it again and again. What do you think the net effect is? That's right, it makes these negative emotional habit patterns all that much harder to change, much less reverse.

People who have a very pronounced anger management issue are actually chasing a high. They're not going to tell you. Often times this is completely foreign to them, but that's what's going on. And that's why it's so easy for them to just snap. It's so easy for them to just go down that emotional rabbit hole again and again and again.

Make no mistake about it, people who engage in this emotional pattern of editing their personal reality are getting something in the end. There is some sort of reward, and this becomes very addictive.

I know this is unpleasant. In fact, to a lot of people, it might even be downright uncomfortable, but we need to get real. If this is your situation, own up to it. Otherwise, you're not going to get better. Otherwise, your anger is always going to get the better of you and you will overreact in the worst way possible.

At this point, I want you to reread all the previous chapters because starting in Chapter 6, we're going to focus on the solution. Unfortunately, if you are unclear about any concept that I have presented up to this point, Chapter 6 and succeeding chapters are not going to make a whole lot of sense to you.

This is a good time to go back to previous chapters, read them thoroughly, recap them, and then move on to the next chapter. Give yourself the time and the space to do this properly. Otherwise, you're just stuffing your mind full of data which ultimately won't help you all that much.

For this information to help you, you have to see the big picture. You have to see how all of these fit together so you can understand the kind of emotional re-engineering you need to do to achieve real progress. See you in the next chapter.

Chapter 6: How to Control Your Anger without Drugs

A lot of people deal with anger and other issues involving extreme emotions the easy way. There I said it. Make no mistake about it taking mood-altering or mellowing drugs is the easier way to handle extreme emotions. If you easily get triggered and your emotions often get the better of you,

I really can't blame you for taking anti-anxiety medication, mood-altering legal prescription drugs or recreational drugs. A lot of people smoke marijuana because they want to mellow out. They want to chill. Without weed, their emotions often get the better of them. They're sick of it so they just self-medicate.

In fact, I know a lot of people who do this. When I was in college, one of the coolest guys I knew smoked a lot of weed, and it was easy to see why because he can't go a few days without pot because he gets really angry. He's a very emotional person. He reacts easily to even the slightest disappointment, slightest negativity, and he always has to judge people, situations, and things. He has to always have the final word.

As you can well imagine, hanging out with such a person is what a lot of people would call "an acquired taste". He was a dear friend of mine, and what made it really easy to hang out with him was when he was stoned, which was pretty much one-third to one-half the time. He's a completely different person. He was just chill. In fact, he would be the mellowest person in the room. Everybody's just pumped up. It's easy for people to get all emotional as a group, but he would always be the anchor of sensibility and reason in a large part due to all that THC floating through his bloodstream.

Drugs are definitely one way to deal with emotional issues. As you can well imagine, it's not the optimal way. What if you have to operate heavy machinery? What if you have to drive? What if you have to be around children? Do you see the problem here?

Legal mood-altering drugs like antidepressants, anti-anxiety medications are not any better either. The side effects can be quite formidable. We're talking about sexual dysfunction, lack of appetite or increased appetite. There have been also many claims regarding suicidal thoughts.

Make no mistake about going with legal medication is not a slam dunk either. What if I told you that you can control your anger without drugs? You're probably rolling your eyes, you're probably even laughing out loud but it's absolutely true. You don't have to mellow out with medication.

Here's an overview. You need to go through the following steps. If you go through these the correct way, you will be able to get out from under your anger. I know this all seems too good to be true at this stage. You're probably reeling from the tremendous force of your anger. It's like almost irresistible.

I understand that but let me tell you if you do these steps and you follow everything correctly, it will improve your ability to manage your anger. In fact, you would be able to control it to the point where your life can become so much better, and the best part to all of this is that it doesn't involve any kind of self-deception, electric shock, mind-altering drugs or any extreme measures.

Instead, it all involves you taking more active control over your thought patterns. A lot of people have a tough time with this because this requires effort, attention, and energy. The good news here is you don't have to be a hero. You don't have to achieve miraculous results right out of the gate. By simply trying over and over again in simple steps, eventually, you will get there. What's important is consistency.

Here's an overview of the steps:

- ✓ Be clear about this situation
- ✓ Select what you're emotionally focusing on
- ✓ Understand what you've emotionally focused on

- ✓ Choose to resolve things positively
- ✓ Choose to channel your focus on learning
- ✓ Use diffusion steps
- ✓ Choose to read the situation under the best light possible
- ✓ Focus on the negative consequences if you act in anger

This overview spells out the key lessons that you will learn. These are specific actions you need to take. None of these are optional. You have to go through this process step by step. This is sequential.

I'm not expecting you to master all these steps the first time around. It's usually a better idea to stick to one step and keep practicing it until you master it. Once you are comfortable with that step, and it happens naturally for you, you can go on to the next step. Master that and then you move on.

Don't think for a second that you have to race through this. There is no race to run here. You're not competing against anybody else. Just because you're going through this at a pace that you think is too slow doesn't mean that there's something wrong with you.

We're all different people. We're wired differently. We have different experiences. Accordingly, we go through new materials based on our own personal speed.

Given that you are essentially dealing with your emotions and how you process the stimuli that you pick out from the rest of the world, you are entitled to your pace. Nobody can call you out for being slow. Nobody can hold you to some sort of timeline. I need to make this clear so you don't put any unnecessary pressure on yourself. Again, this is not a race.

Even if you take baby steps forward, that's still good news. How come? Baby steps forward are still steps forward. You're still headed in the right direction.

Access your FREE Report

Before you read further, I would like to thank you for downloading this book.

As a way of showing my appreciation, I want to give you a **FREE REPORT** along with this book.

Free Report: 4 Amazing Techniques That Will Help You to Control Your Anger!

This Free Report will teach you about-

- 4 Techniques to Control Your Anger.
- Stop Being A Complainer: I'll Show How

- The Power of Forgiveness.
- Why You Should Practice Forgiveness.
- Avoid Anxiety & Stress using 5 Simple Tips.

Please visit the below link to access this FREE Report!

http://geni.us/freeanger

Chapter 7: Be Clear About the Situation

As I mentioned in my description of people's emotional rollercoaster, you perceive certain things or certain mental images flash in your mind. When this happens, choose to be absolutely clear about the situation. Ask yourself "What exactly is going on here?" A lot of people do not ask this question. They just jump in with both feet.

For example, they look at a situation with ten different things going on. The moment they see two things present, they automatically assume everything else. They couldn't care less if other things are happening. Instead, they just assume that if these two things are happening, this is what's actually happening. If these two things are present, this is actually what's happening. In other words, they're assuming.

Don't be surprised if things blow up in your face because you assume things that were simply not there. It pays to look at the facts. Instead of jumping to conclusions instinctively about the situation, pay attention to facts.

This is more difficult than you think because as you get older, you think that you have become smarter when you do this.

When it comes to picking up new instructions, this is how adults usually do things. They look at a new set of instructions and always refer it to the stuff they already know. If they see enough familiar items, they quickly connect the dots to try to move on because our minds are very efficient.

Usually, this pays off, but when it comes to your emotions, oftentimes it doesn't. It pays to actually step back, slow down and look at the whole situation clearly. Pay attention to the facts that are happening. In other words, ask yourself, "Is this what I think is happening? What exactly is going on here?" Don't be afraid to ask if you're not sure.

Pick apart the situation. When journalists go to a crime scene or are reporting on a news item, ethical and professional journalists go through "the reporters' questions." What are these questions? Who, what, where, when, why, how. They ask the basics. They ask for facts.

You should do the same. Don't ask conclusions from yourself. Instead, pick apart the situation. What exactly is going on? Who is involved? What happened? How many things happened? Where did this take place? When? Is there anything else going on? How did these things become related to each other? Then and only then should you consider the idea of why.

Unfortunately, a lot of people only need to look at a few things and then they jump onto why. In other words, they impose a conclusion on something they perceive. This is how they edit their reality. This is their analytical process.

I hope you can see how dangerous that type of thinking can be. You may be seeing things that are not there. You may be reading in details that are not there. How accurate do you think your conclusion will be if it's based on faulty premises?

Do Yourself a Favor and Look at the Whole Thing

If you're dealing with a memory, look at what happened. If you have just experienced something right now, look at the whole thing. Don't just obsess about the most stressful part.

Sure, somebody gave you a bad look or somebody said a mean word to you. I understand that. That's the most stressful part but pay attention to the whole context. Look at what happened before, during and after the stressful part. These are important details.

Take a Quick Look at Consequences

Now that this has played out or now that you perceive certain things from the past, take a look at the consequences. Ask yourself what is the worst-case scenario if you reacted in the worst way possible? This doesn't take a rocket scientist to figure out. In fact, a lot of people focus on this. This is the most familiar to them.

Now, I want you to flip the script. Look at the situation from the other extreme. What is the best-case scenario that can happen if you reacted in the best way? Again, this doesn't take much imagination. The answer is usually nothing. You were happy before, you are happy after. Sure, there was something stressful that happened in the middle, but you don't have to react in the worst way. You don't have to feel bad.

To paraphrase Eleanor Roosevelt, nobody can make you feel lousy without your consent. They may have the worst malice in the world for you, but if you do not accept their judgment of you or their definition or perception of the situation, then none of that would matter to you. You can happily go your own way.

Just because people say bad things or do bad things doesn't necessarily mean that you have nothing to say about it. You can reject. You can choose to look at things in the best way possible. You can ignore.

Of course, some of these responses are more productive than others, but you get my point. Don't think that just because something happens that there is really no other way to read it except in the worst way possible. If you do this, you're essentially feeding the beast. You are making the negative emotional habit you have with anger worse and worse.

The payoff is there. You get that release, but so is the harsh, emotional reality. The worst part? This gets easier and easier and easier because it becomes second nature to you.

What's really happening is you're going down a downward spiral. Eventually, you reach a point where anything would basically trigger you, and you become a very miserable person. It's like you're living in your own personal prison with invisible walls.

It doesn't have to be that way. Take a quick look at the consequences both from the worst end and the best-case scenario and understand that there is actually quite a leeway here. This is the reality that there's quite a stretch of possibilities here. You're not trapped. You're not forced to feel miserable when you detect certain elements. Feeling negative is not a foregone conclusion.

Use Your Mind, Not Your Heart

I know this is one of those things that are easier said than done. I'm sure you've heard this before in different contexts.

Sure, we all know that we should use our mind, not our hearts. We all know that we should respond to life in a rational and logical way instead of doing things emotionally or impulsively.

There are a lot of things that we know we should do, but we don't do them. Why? Because we feel that we must do other things. While a lot of things make intellectual sense on a practical level, we don't get around to doing them because we don't develop a sense of urgency towards it.

Most people know what they should be doing. Most people know what kind of issues they need to resolve so they can live happier lives but, unfortunately, most people still continue to plod along. Most are still frustrated, angry or even in denial.

Make no mistake about it using your mind not your heart is very hard because you're bucking against a habit. You're used to responding and reacting in the worst way possible. How do you push back against that?

The good news here is that it may be hard, but it is doable with enough practice. Seriously. Start low and slow. It doesn't have to be big. You don't have to be a hero. You don't have to create some sort of black-and-white contrast between what you were doing before and how you respond now.

Use your mind, not your heart. Eventually, you will get there. Eventually, it would be big enough so it's self-sustaining. It's in a way working against emotional habits.

It's very similar to water dripping on a hard rock in a cave. If you see this, you're probably going to be thinking there's no way that water is going to erode that rock. I mean that rock's really hard. It's tough, it's immovable and this water is just too soft. It is, after all, water, and there's not enough of it. It's not like it's pouring on the rock. It's just dripping. Every few seconds, it's dripping.

Well, let me tell you to get back to that rock in twenty years. What do you think you will see? That's right. That rock either has a hole somewhere in the top portion of it or it has been weathered smooth by the water.

Consistent effort is all you need. You don't have to set yourself up with unrealistic expectations of overnight results. If you're going to be using your mind, not your heart to look at the facts that trigger your anger, you need to be consistent.

The good news here is that as long as you start, regardless of how low and how slow, it will be okay. It's kind of like raising up a car with a tire jack. It may be a small increment, but the good news is when you jack it up, it's not going to go down unless you release the jack. Sure, it seems like you're not really moving all that much, but that's okay.

Just like when water from the ceiling of a cave drips on a rock, it's not really doing all that much, but as long as that water drips consistently and as long as you pop the jack consistently no matter how small, no matter how seemingly insignificant, you will make an impact.

Use your mind to look at your complete situation to pick apart the facts. This way, you won't jump to conclusions. This way, you won't imagine things that are not there.

Chapter 8: Select What You're Emotionally Focusing On

Now that you have a clear idea of what exactly is going on, and you have full situational awareness because you're focusing on facts, the next step is to go from mental to emotional.

In Chapter 7, you were focused on what you mentally perceived. This is what you think you're seeing. Now, we're going to zero in on the facts that you are emotionally dwelling on. Believe it or not, the facts that you choose to focus on can make matters worse or defuse it. Indeed, these facts impact how you choose to read the situation.

Let me tell you a personal story. I went to a club in college with a lot of friends of mine. There were about eight of us in the group. We go to this part of the club where there were a lot of really hot women. I'm talking about blond-haired, blue-eyed, mid-western, hot, all-American chicks. These women had legs that went on for miles, amazing bodies and really bubbly personalities.

Well, at one point, one of the girls looked at me from about five feet and started laughing. I kind of emotionally blanked out. I was the only non-Caucasian dude there. Everybody else was white, by white, I'm talking about Spanish, Italian, Scandinavian, Irish or of English stock. All-American. I was the only non-Caucasian guy there.

So, I thought that I was the issue. I thought she was picking on the fact that I stood out. It's kind of like looking at a picture and saying to yourself what doesn't fit here? As you can tell, I was pretty sensitive about that. I just dwelled on her laugh and the fact that she was looking in my general direction. She was five feet away. She was looking ahead, and she was laughing. I automatically assumed that she was laughing at me because I was the only non-white dude there.

As you can tell, I was pretty upset. I was like she's judging me, and then it gets worse and worse. I started feeling ugly. I started feeling that I was unwanted, that I had no business being there. What do you think the effect was on my efforts to talk to her friends?

It felt like I was fish out of water because I was stuck in a negative spiral of my own doing. I was judging the situation in the worst way possible so I was trying to lay out some lines, trying to get some game and I was failing because I already thought I was a failure. I feared that these people were judging me, that they thought that I didn't belong there.

So, it corroded my self-confidence. It was a double whammy. It hit my self-esteem, and it hit my self-confidence, and I'm sorry to report but that night ended with a big fat zero for me. Absolutely no play. Nada. Zilch. A total loss.

What made matters worse was that for many years, I would think about that, and it would eat into my confidence, at least when it came to women who fit that profile. I would do well with Latina, Asian, Middle Eastern women or Persian women, but mid-Western chicks, no chance. It's as if something clicked in my head and my game just fell apart.

Well, five years after that, my friends and I had a reunion of sorts. It was really just a glorified drinking party, and one of the guys brought back that story of us going to that bar and him doing something really stupid and getting a lot of laughs from the chicks. I was not aware that he was doing stuff behind me. So, I was just looking at this really good-looking blond female, I really thought she was a goddess, she was that hot, laughing at who I thought was me. It turned out she was laughing at my friend behind me.

However, I was so emotionally focused on the laugh, and gave it so much meaning that actually made matters worse. How come? Well, if I was not so emotionally focused on her laugh and packing in so many negative meanings, I could have looked around and seen my friend who was wearing a jockstrap.

That's right. He was wearing his underwear and his jockstrap on his head, making a total ass of himself, and all the chicks were laughing. He did it on purpose. He was the class clown.

However, I was completely clueless about that until we met five years later and guess what happened? All those negative memories vaporized because now, I saw that I was emotionally focusing on the wrong things. I was pouring emotional gasoline or charcoal and making things worse. I was reading the situation in the worst way possible.

It's really important to understand that you must be conscious of the part of the event or the scene in your memory that you focus on the most. It's not enough to be clear as to the facts; you also need to focus on what a specific aspect meant.

Let me tell you even if I turned around and my friend making an ass out of himself, I may still have walked away with a negative read of the situation because of the emotional focus I was a putting on that chick's laugh. The woman was laughing in a very hearty way. I thought she was judging me. She was condemning me. I packed on all the negative readings that I could. Be mindful of the part of the event or scene that you emotionally to focus on because your emotions are doing you in.

If I had this magical rewind button and I find myself back in that scene, there would be a totally different memory because I would just look back and see that these guys were horsing around behind me and then I probably would laugh at them as well and when I see that female laughing in my general direction, I can see that, instead of a judgment, as an opportunity because are responding emotionally the same way.

In fact, my friend told me that he knew another guy who actually dated that chick, and it turned out that she thought I was a pretty cute Polynesian-looking dude, and she was kind of wondering why I was giving her the cold shoulder. Funny how that works, right?

Be aware of the part of the scene or event that you focus on. You might be opening yourself up to all the worst readings when it actually doesn't match up with reality. How do you solve this? How you get out from under this?

Pick Your Focus Consciously

Look at the scene that's playing out. Pick a part you can read in a positive way. For example, if a girl is laughing at you or in your general direction, look at the part where you can read in a positive way. The fact that she's now looking at you eye to eye, that's a clue. She's laughing in your general direction, but it may not be you she's laughing at. So, read this in a positive way.

Alternatively, you can pick a part of the scene that you can emotionally master. This is the part that triggers you the least. The fact that they laughed and then they did not look at you straight in the eye and looked at somebody else, focus on that.

This doesn't mean that you should deny the rest of the picture. This doesn't mean that you somehow hypnotize yourself and impose some sort of alternative reality on what happened.

Instead, I'm inviting you to look at the big picture, and make sure that you are purposeful and conscious regarding your emotional focus. This enables you to gain something extremely important: perspective.

Even if you are dealing with a situation that is negative, it doesn't have to be as negative as you think. It doesn't have to be a complete and total disaster. Oftentimes, what we may perceive as negativity can actually be positive. It all depends on what perspective we focus on.

Chapter 9: Understand What You're Emotionally Focused On

In the previous chapter, I was talking about understanding what it is you are so emotionally focused on. In this chapter, you're going to focus on understanding just what it is you are dwelling on. In the previous case, you were trying to wrap your mind around what exactly is going on. In other words, you're looking at facts. You're looking at how things actually played out. You are trying to get an accurate idea of things as they are.

In this chapter, your task is to see if your understanding of it actually meets its reality. In other words, in the previous chapter, we focused on accuracy based on facts. Now, you're trying to square your impression of the scene.

You have to understand these are two all the different things. What you think something is, is different from what it actually is. Now, things get really rough when you're emotionally focused on something based on what you think it is.

Again, you're reading all sorts of things into it. You're assuming all sorts of stuff. It turns out that it's not accurate. It turns out that you're missing certain aspects. You may be reading too much into it or you're leaving out a lot of things. Whatever the case maybe you end up at the wrong place.

You have to ask yourself this central question. Is it what I think it is? Please pay attention to this question. Pick it apart. Basically, you already have something in mind. This calls your attention to your prejudices or preconceptions. You are aware that this is happening. You wake up to the fact that you are reading stuff into the situation.

So, when you ask yourself, "Is it what I think it is?" you are actually asking two questions. "What is it" and "What do I think of it?"

Coming in, you already have an impression. The question is does the reality of the thing that you are obsessing about or worrying about line up to what you think about it.

A lot of people blast through this. They really do. They don't even go through this analysis, and this is why they stumble headlong into the same negative vortex of anger and other raw, negative emotions. It doesn't have to be that way. By simply taking a step back and asking yourself, "Is it what I think it is?" should be enough to awaken certain parts of your logical and reasoning faculties to at least pay attention to the facts.

Stay Anchored to Facts

Make no mistake about it your brain operates on so many different levels, and it does things so quickly. It's as if you jump straight to a conclusion. You only need to detect certain things. In fact, you may even have a fuzzy impression that those things are actually present, and you just jump to the worst conclusions possible. You're emotional. You are holding back from saying what's on top of your mind, which is not all that positive.

What if you just chilled out and took a step back and ask yourself, "Is this what I think it is?" Not only do you get clued into what you are judging the situation as, but you also remind yourself to look at the facts. Because if you do this, you end up asking yourself whether the facts back up what you think it is.

Again, you have to assume a reporter's mindset. Don't just get taken emotionally by something happening or a memory that flashes in your mind.

Focus on WHAT actually happened.

Focus on other things that were going on when something happened.

During this time, there are many other things going on. Be aware of them. How do they relate to the thing that you you're dwelling on?

For example, in the story I raised in Chapter 8, the hot blonde laughing at me, that took place in context. There were other women around her who were also laughing, and they were not looking my direction. They looked up, and then they looked to the side. Some were covering their mouths, and others were actually leaning to the side of me because I was blocking their view.

If I had only focused on those other elements that took place within that same time period, it would have been obvious that this hot chick was not laughing at me. They were laughing at something happening behind me. Unfortunately, I only learned about this five years later. However, I would have made things so much easier on myself as well as my ego and self-esteem if I had only focused on what other things were going on when those things were taking place.

Be Clear on How Something Turned Out

As you see something take place in front of you or in your memory, be clear as to the process that took place. What happened before, during and after? How did this these flow into each other? Were there any special processes involved? Were there any more data or inputs involved?

Clearly Identify Who is Involved

Believe it or not a lot of people get all worked up about memories involving shadows. They're not really clear as to who said what or who did what, but the conclusion in their minds at least is very clear. In fact, it's black and white. They feel bad because they're fat. They feel bad because they "look funny." They feel humiliated about something somebody said, but they can't quite put their finger on who said what and when exactly.

Don't Just Jump to the Question of Why

Unfortunately, people blast through this whole process because they just want to get to why. They want to get to the explanation as quickly as possible. A lot of people are under the impression that this is effective efficient thinking. Absolutely wrong.

Instead, this is sloppy thinking because you're not really dealing with the facts. You just jumped in because you had the worst-case conclusion already. You're asking yourself a loaded question. If anything, you're just going through the emotions.

You're not really trying to unpack everything. You're not trying to untangle these facts.

Instead, you just want to go straight to why. However, you already know the answer. The answer is we are tempted to automatically assign intent.

Sure, again, going back to my story. This hot blonde with blue eyes was laughing at me. A very slim, athletic body. Amazing package. So, I automatically assign intent. She was laughing at me because I didn't belong there. I was a fish out of the water. I did not fit in and on and on the list of bad intentions go.

Unfortunately, I gave into the temptation right there and then and whenever that memory flashed into my mind for those five years until everything was explained to me. I felt bad. I felt bad about myself. I just jumped to the worst interpretation whatsoever and read into her action intention.

Believe it or not, people can laugh at you, and it doesn't have to be with bad intent. Maybe you're cracking a joke or maybe they're laughing at the situation. You can't always assume that when people do something involving or impacting you that it is with the worst intentions in the world.

Regardless, if you do this, your emotions will get the better of you. If you keep doing this over and over again, you will always read into people's often neutral actions the worst intent possible.

What do you think the effect will be on your self-esteem? How do you think your self-confidence will be affected? The answer should be obvious.

Chapter 10: Choose to Resolve Things Positively

When you do the steps outlined in Chapter 8 and 9, you get emotional space. You at least slow things down so you can gain some sort of perspective. You need to do this because the more space you have to work with, the higher the chance you can resolve the mental image or your reading of whatever is happening in front of you in a more positive way. You have to consciously and purposely decide to resolve or deal with the situation or memory positively. Now, this is easy to say; it's very hard to do.

Please understand that this is not a whim. This is not something that you just randomly choose to do. This is definitely not an impulse like something that hits you. It's not something that you do when you feel like it. No. This must be purposeful. In fact, you must view it as a commitment. You have to take it to that level.

Anything short of that will not produce positive results. Far from it. We know what we should be doing, but we often find all sorts of excuses not to do it. That's part of human nature. That's why we stumble again and again.

This has to be purposeful. You have to do this because you committed to it.

Really successful people don't let their situations throw them off. Now, they get emotionally disturbed just like everybody else, but they find the emotional space to deal with the situation based on their ideal standards, not their emotions. In other words, they always remember how they should respond.

Instead of letting their emotions get the better of them and just reacting as quickly as possible, they focus on their standards. Again, this is not easy. However, the more you do this and fail, the closer you get to success.

You have to keep doing it. It has to be something you do out of commitment. Not because it feels right. Not because it feels good. Not because you feel that you have some time or some opportunity to do it. Instead, you do it over and over again.

Focus on Your Ideal Standards

Once you've created that emotional space, and you have committed to responding based on your ideal standards, what exactly would you focus on? Well, you have to ask yourself, "What are my highest values?"

Do I treat people with respect? Do I treat people like the way I want to be treated? Do I seek to understand people first before I demand to be understood? Do I look at the situation with an open mind because that's who I am? Am I a person of high moral values? Do I try to always find the best in people?

Find your highest values and then ask yourself, "Am I dealing with these facts based on these values? Am I sticking to them? Am I choosing to respond based on my values and ideals regardless of how bad it feels?

Right now, you're feeling like you just want to give this person a piece of your mind. This person annoyed you or this person is actually making you angry. What do you do? Do you turn to your values and allow them to guide you, or do you just do what comes naturally?

Let me tell you most people would just do what comes naturally and, unfortunately, when you do that, you end up burning bridges. You also end up creating enemies. You might think that this person already is an enemy. Well, guess what? This person will become a bigger enemy in the future.

This is not easy because sometimes people say and do certain things that humiliate you. It's hard because you're feeling that if you do not give them a piece of your mind or you push back in the worst way possible, you're losing out. Your pride hurts.

Well, here's the thing. If this is all a commitment to you, then you are going to have to override these emotions. You're going to have to do this not because it feels good. Obviously, it doesn't. Instead, you're going to have to overcome these all-too-natural emotions involving pushback, revenge, payback, and everything else because of your standards. You hold yourself up to a higher level of values.

This is the test. Are you really that kind of person, or are you just like everybody else? Do you do stuff that is quick and easy, or do you take the high road? It really all boils down to commitment. You're going to have to respond based on what you committed to.

Again, none of this is easy but let me tell you it may be rough at first, but the more you do this, the easier it will become. I'm not saying that you will ultimately reach a point where this just happens on autopilot. That's not going to happen. We're all human beings. We all have feelings.

However, the good news is with enough practice, things become much easier. I'm not saying that it's never going to sting or it's never going to get annoying or slightly irritating, but it's going to be very manageable. It's definitely going to be better than the now where you are faced with a seemingly irresistible urge to just hit somebody across the jaw or curse them out or remind them of nasty stuff they did in the past.

I know you're hurt. Understand that feeling is not permanent. Commitment, on the other hand, based on your highest ideals can be permanent. You have a choice to make.

Chapter 11: Choose to Channel Your Focus on Learning

I know this is to say and, believe me, a lot of the instructions in this book are easier said than done, but this is probably one of the more difficult sections of this book. It's easy to say that we should focus on learning. It's easy to think that while we cannot avoid losing, we don't have to necessarily lose the lesson.

I mean that's cute, and it definitely makes sense, but let's get real here. Stuff that makes sense intellectually or at the level of our minds doesn't automatically make sense when it comes to our feelings, emotions, impulses and day-to-day actions.

Regardless, you're going to have to do this. As frustrating as emotionally charged situations or mental images from the past may be, they can be very productive. It's very hard because if you are a victim of abuse in the past, you can't help but get emotional, and it's a negative rollercoaster ride.

You have to try to turn things around. Depending on how traumatic the memory may be, it would take more time, but it can be done. You can turn things around so it's so what would have been negative experiences now and negative memories can yield something productive.

You can Choose to Learn

Learning is a choice, and this choice requires us to channel our focus. We have to redirect our focus from getting even, feeling miserable, feeling less of a person to choose to learn from it.

What can You Possibly Learn from Negative Triggers or Experiences?

Well, here is just a short list. This is by no means the complete list, but there's a lot here. You can learn the following:

What Triggers You

The most obvious things that you can learn from your daily trying experiences, as well as your difficult memories, are your triggers. What exactly triggers you? Is it a mental image? Is it certain said words? Do things have to combine in such a way for you to become emotionally triggered? Pay attention to these because the more details you have, the easier it would be for you to unpack your triggers.

I'm not saying that you will automatically take out their sting, but you can definitely make them a little blunter so they don't tear into you. Eventually, it can get so round and so light that they do little to no damage. However, for that happen, you have to be clear as to what exactly triggers you.

How Does Your Emotional Rollercoaster Play Out Specifically?

The emotional rollercoaster I described in an earlier chapter is real, but it plays out in different ways for different people. Again, this comes with the territory because we all have different experiences. We come from different walks of life. We have different backgrounds, different childhoods, all these differences, of course, add up to quite a bit.

So, focus on what makes your particular personal emotional rollercoaster ride. How does it play out? What happens before, during and after?

How You Can Disrupt Your Rollercoaster

Now that you have a fairly clear idea of how otherwise neutral stimuli you pick up from the world leads to you saying the wrong things, thinking things that hurt you or stress you out or actually doing things that make worse, the next step is to figure out how to get off the rollercoaster.

How can you disrupt it? Do you need to breathe? Do you need to turn away? Do you need to focus on another set of facts? Do you believe thinking of another memory can disrupt it? Regardless, you need to throw these things around.

It's kind of like throwing pasta against the wall. Many times, a lot of the stuff will bounce off, but if you keep doing it, something will stick. So, ask yourself how can I disrupt my personal emotional rollercoaster? You're not doomed to ride it. It doesn't have to keep playing out the same sad way over and over again.

The good news here is that the more you try to get off the rollercoaster, the closer to success you will be. What's important is you've tried. It may not work the first few times, but you keep doing it. Again, it's like throwing spaghetti at the wall. Eventually, you will be able to disrupt it.

Become Aware of Your Emotional Attention Span

What if I told you that the most humiliating, degrading, crushing memory only flashes its intense emotions for a fairly short period of time? Now, don't get me wrong. I understand that when you go through those memories that flash through your mind, it feels like forever. Believe me, I know exactly with you're talking about because that happened to me.

This doesn't take away from the fact that these intense emotions don't last forever; otherwise, you go crazy. That's how much resources they take. That's how stressful these are for your mental and emotional faculties.

By choosing to become aware of how long you are engaged by negative emotions, you give yourself hope. You quickly realize that your negative states of mind because you got triggered by a memory or by something that just took place won't last forever. Isn't that good news?

It's kind of like watching this really dark cloud up ahead. Sure, it's going to be measurable under that cloud because it's raining, but it's going to pass by. Actually, if you look at the sky during storms, the clouds are actually moving really fast.

By focusing on your emotional attention span, you allow yourself to be more hopeful because deep down inside, you know this is not permanent. This will blow over. As intense and raw as it may feel right now, my anger will blow over.

The Facts as They Are

Another thing you can learn from moments of intense anger are the facts of what trigger you. You can actually pay attention to what actually happened. This is a big deal because often people just pay attention to two facts and everything else is assumed. They just fill in the rest of the picture.

When you focus on the facts, you quickly realize that it's not as black and white as you think. Just as it's easy for you to get worked up by certain parts, other facts might point to other conclusions. You'd feel better if you took those facts and ran with them.

The Facts as You Perceive Them

Another thing you could learn is how your mind perceives things. You start looking at the association between certain facts and your conclusions. If you keep repeating this enough time, you probably would start laughing at yourself. You would say, "Oh, well, that's how I think. Talk about making things worse for myself. I'm not going to do that again."

You have to allow yourself to reach that level. Instead of calling yourself, "Oh, I'm an idiot for thinking that. Oh, I'm a total loser." No, you just say, "Okay, that's how I used to do things, and it leads to a bad place. Now I know and I am now aware that these facts do not have to lead to the end of the world. I don't have to make such a big deal out of them. I don't have to go on the deep end."

You can Learn to Stick to Your Values

Finally, you can learn how to stick to your values regardless of your emotional state. This is probably the best lesson you can learn. Truly classy people are able to maintain their dignity despite the emotional fire and explosion raging within them. It's not easy, but once you choose to learn from situations that normally trigger you, you will be able to achieve internal control, and this, of course, happens when you act out of commitment.

Turbocharge Your Personal Anger Management Learning Cycle by Doing the Following:

Please understand that the list of things I've described above is hard to learn because that's a lot of stuff to keep track of. Make things easier on yourself by doing the following:

First, you need to keep a journal. You don't have to be a novelist. You don't have to write really long passages. Just keep track of your emotions. Keep track of what happened and how you responded to it. Focus on the facts. Try to list out the things that you could learn from the situation.

Next, track your progress. Again, this is easier to do if you keep a journal. It would be great if you are aware that after a few months, it takes a lot to trigger you. In fact, the moment you become aware of that, things become easier because you can draw hope and confidence from that. You would quickly realize that you don't have to assume the worst. You don't have to emotionally lose control. You have it in you to respond to your highest values.

Finally, when you read your journal and you compare where you are now with where you began, you cannot help but feel hopeful. Really. You end up encouraging yourself because you realize how far you've come. You may not be in a perfect situation, and you will still definitely be far away from perfect, but you're so much better than when you started.

You need to keep a journal. It doesn't have to be a physical journal. It doesn't have to be a book or a planner you can leaf through. It can be a simple electronic document that to you keep on your mobile phone or tablet or laptop.

Regardless, you need to find a way to record your journey, track your progress and inspire yourself constantly. You have to encourage yourself because you are engaged in something very big and profound. Most people are unable to do this because they don't give themselves the chance to do it.

You're doing something big because if you are able to tame and redirect your anger, the world opens up to you. It no longer has to consist of one disappointment after another or one missed opportunity after another.

Emotional control and self-control, in general, can lead to greater success across the board. I'm talking about all areas of your life. Get that journal going and start focusing on the lessons you're learning.

Chapter 12: Use These Steps to Defuse Your Anger

At this stage, you should have enough situational awareness regarding what you're perceiving and how you are reacting to your perception. You have arrived at a very important stage. This is quite a victory. Pat yourself on the back. Allow yourself to feel good about your accomplishment because, let's face it, most people don't get this far.

The moment they see certain patterns, they fly off the handle. In fact, most people don't even need to see all that many facts. They automatically assume the worst or believe that they understand what's going on and it's the worst situation ever and they have a tried and proven reaction. On and on it goes.

You have finally made a breakthrough by refusing to handle things that way. Now, you have situational awareness. You're focused on the facts. Even after all this progress, it's really important to use certain techniques that would enable you to defuse any leftover anger. While you are in a position where most of your anger properly dealt with, there's still quite a bit of raw, negative emotions to work with.

Don't be surprised by this because if you have been dealing with certain stresses by over-reacting, it's going to take some time to get over old habits. You should already understand that you can't change overnight. It's perfectly okay to have some anger left over.

The question then becomes, "How do we deal with this anger?" You may have reduced it quite a bit because now, you're emotionally and situationally aware. You are more objective in your assessments of situations. But that can only take you so far. We are, after all, creatures of habit. We have grown accustomed to emotionally dealing with things a certain way. It's not like you're going to snap out of it overnight.

Use the following techniques that I will teach you to defuse your anger. They're quite eclectic. Mix and match them based on how well they fit your personality. Try to use them at least several times and then you will figure out which works the best for you. The worst thing that you can do is to not try them at all and just assume that one is better than the other.

I suggest that you try them all at least several times each and then you will see a pattern. You will be able to pick which techniques produce the best results and you can stick to those and improve upon them. Take them to the next level so you can get better results. Regardless of what you do, you need to use these.

Why do You Need to Defuse Your Anger?

Like I always say, to get people to do something, it's not enough to focus on what they should be doing. Instead, I want to clearly explain why you need to do it. I hope you'll be motivated by these benefits. So why do this?

First of all, when you use these tried and proven techniques to defuse your anger, your rational side can override your emotional side. Like I mentioned earlier, your emotional side works like a roller coaster. Once you detect certain things and you give a stimuli a certain reading, your mental processes are like trying to hit the brakes on a train that's going top speed. It's going to take a long time for things to slow down.

As much as you try to use your rational side, you're going to be at a serious disadvantage. When you use the techniques below to defuse your anger, it makes it so much easier for your rational side to overcome the more emotional aspect of your personality.

Another benefit you get from these techniques is that you would be able to establish quite a bit of emotional distance. At this point, you should be able to do this already, but you can really take things to the next level by using the following simple techniques.

Finally, using these steps enables you to achieve higher and greater levels of clarity. Eventually, you will get used to expecting this level of clarity and this can become a new habit that can displace your bad emotional habits. Instead of quickly and almost instantly becoming angry, you crave clarity. This becomes your default response.

This doesn't mean that you might not get angry later on, but at least you ask yourself, "Is everything clear enough?" That becomes your first response and believe me, that is a tremendous breakthrough because once you achieve that level of clarity, you can widen it, deepen it and eventually, you can choose to overcome your anger and deal with a situation in a more productive way.

Method #1: Breathe

Did you know that by simply breathing, you can defuse psychological, emotional and physical tension? That's right. Just fill up your lungs and you will achieve some relaxation. Once you have done the previous steps outlined in prior chapters, you need to learn how to use your breath to increase your chances of greater levels of emotional clarity and distance. You need these to get out from under the heavy weight of your anger habit. Make no mistake about it. It's a habit.

How do you breathe properly? There are many different ways to do this. They can all be boiled down into 3 major techniques.

First, you can choose to do rapid deep breaths. You basically huff and puff really quickly. What's important is that you breathe deeply. This way, you oxygenate your blood, you pump a lot more oxygen to your brain and this can lead to greater clarity. A lot of people would rather do this than the other types of breathing because this is more in line with their emotional state.

When you are in a situation and people laugh at you or somebody that annoys you does something that really ticks you off, you're probably already starting to breathe rapidly. When you deepen that rapid breathing, you can relax. This is already more in line with how you're already responding.

Another approach would be to slow down and take deep, long breaths. You're not pausing between breaths, you're just deepening it. You breathe in deeply and slowly and then you shift and breathe out deeply and slowly. You keep repeating this until a sense of calm descends upon you. The sensation usually starts at the back of your head. It works down your neck and if you keep this up long enough, it makes its way to the front of your brain.

Whatever route your breath takes, keep breathing deeply. The downside to this approach is that it requires you to slow down. When you are heated or caught in the moment, this is not always easy, but it's definitely worth trying.

Finally, you can breathe deeply and slowly and then pause each breath. You can pause for about 4-10 seconds, then you breathe in again, pause for 4-10 seconds, then breathe out again and repeat this process. This is actually the most powerful, but you have to actively slow down. Like I said earlier, often times when you're heated, it's like trying to stop a runaway train. It's just too heavy and intense.

The good news here is if you apply any of these breathing techniques, you would be richly rewarded because you would be able to handle what would otherwise be a very explosive situation with a lot more control.

Method #2: Simply Choose to Wait

The next method you can apply is to just wait. That's right. Let time take its course. Now, you may be thinking, "I don't have that much time. This person just called me an idiot." or "That guy who cheated on my wife just showed up. What am I going to do?" Well, believe it or not, that rush of negative emotions that you're feeling is not much different from being caught in a rain storm. If you've ever had that experience, you remember that it feels like it's going to last forever. The rain just keeps falling and it seems to get worse and worse. But what happens eventually?

I don't really care whether you're in Florida or in the tropics or any other part of the world where there's a lot of precipitation and hurricanes or tropical storms, cyclones, monsoons or whatnot. They all lead to the same place. That's right. They all end. You may feel like it will go on forever, but it all ends.

Please understand that just like threatening, menacing storm clouds, this rush of emotion will pass if you allow it. You don't have to jump in with both feet and roll the dice and just give people a piece of your mind. You don't have to let that surge of emotion get the better of you and you get into a fight. You can simply choose to wait it out.

I know that this is not all that appealing to a lot of people. Maybe you're feeling that you have to confront somebody. Maybe you're feeling that you're running away from your problems. You have to understand that you have to use this in conjunction with the other coping mechanisms I'm teaching you in this book. This should be part of your toolbox because when you are able to cultivate this, you become a more patient person. Your ability to control yourself and practice self-discipline grows immensely.

I understand, you're feeling really angry. I understand that it burns. But you'd be surprised as to the sense of strength you feel when you have developed the discipline to simply wait. This isn't easy. It won't happen overnight. But if you keep practicing it, you'd be surprised as to how long your patience becomes.

Method #3: Think of Role Models

Everybody has a role model. Whether we're talking about a famous person, political figure, a family member, a philosophical or spiritual leader. Everybody has somebody they love, respect or admire. When you are facing a really stressful situation and you feel anger boiling up within you, focus on that person that you admire, respect or love. Ask yourself how that person would handle this situation if they were in your place. Put in another way, what would that person's standards be in dealing with this situation.

Regardless of how you do it, hold yourself to that person's standard. This is the secret to this method. Let's face it, when you fly off the handle and you just take care of things because the emotions just hit you and you just can't hold back, you are using your own standards. Let's get real, those standards aren't much because you just let your emotions get the better of you.

By allowing yourself to focus on somebody else's standard, you give yourself a lot of mental power because you may not feel like you are disciplined enough if you were to respond based on your standard, but when you look at somebody you love, respect and admire and try to hold yourself up to their standard, you may have a fighting chance.

Always think of how they would respond. Always think about their thought processes. Alternatively, you can ask yourself, "How would that person view me if they see me get angry easily? How much respect would they have for me if they see me give in to my anger again and again?" Regardless of how you do this, simply shifting your mind to another standard outside of yourself can work wonders. At the very least, it gives you perspective. It also gives you a tremendous amount of emotional distance from your present situation.

Method #4: Focus on Your Ideal Image of Yourself

As I've mentioned previously, we all have our values. We all have certain standards that we think makeup who we are. I need you to remember them.

Next, I want you to create a model from these values. For example, if you value harmony, integrity and unity, do you think yourself as a calm, collected person? Similarly, if you value creativity and individuality, do you think of yourself as a "cool" person worth emulating? I hope you can see the pattern here.

Whatever the case may be, focus on that standard you have of yourself. Again, this is the ideal we're talking about here. This doesn't have to be real. This is your idealized version of who you are. Hold that standard as a model. You understand how upset you are right now. That's not the problem. You can see that clearly.

But, by focusing on that standard model you have of yourself of who you could be if you were living up to your highest ideals, you give yourself a model. You say to yourself, "I don't have to overreact. I don't have to get angry. I don't have to make bad decisions. I don't have to do things that I will come to regret later on. Instead, I know what my ideals are. I know what my standard is."

Focus on the standard. You'll be surprised as to how much resolve and strength you can get by simply looking at the standard that you set for yourself. If anything, it buys you time. It gives you the reserved patience that you need to not blow it.

Method #5: Choose to Channel Your Anger

The next approach is actually one of the toughest. A lot of people really have a tough time with this, but I need to share this with you because this is an option. You probably would need to save this for last. You probably would need to develop quite a bit of discipline first before you step up to this. The good news is it can work for you. I am, of course, talking about channeling.

Here's how it works. First, you absorb the anger and you channel it later. You're not denying that emotion. You're not pretending that it didn't exist. You're not denying yourself. Instead, you absorb the anger. You let the conflict pass, but you hang on to the anger that you feel. On the outside, you look calm, collected and peaceful, but there's anger there. Here's the trick. You're going to have to unload it later. You can't just bottle it up and pretend that it doesn't exist because that's going to lead to a massive and nasty implosion. It's okay to absorb the anger, but you can't store it. These are 2 totally different things.

Eventually, if you store it, people you love, care for and respect will get burned because you will blow up and often times, the blast radius of your raw negative emotions are quite wide. It's okay to absorb the anger, but you need to channel it. How do you channel this raw emotional energy in a very productive way?

Take your pick. You can go to work and pump out all that energy in the form of greater work intensity. For example, I write for a living. When I'm upset with somebody, I choose to be cool about it, but I carry that intensity and express it in the form of greater fiction or greater plot lines. I allow myself to be more energized when I'm researching stuff for my non-fiction work.

Use that energy to work for you instead of constantly working against you. Instead of it corroding your inner core, it can be a source of energy. Similarly, if you play sports, channel that anger in the form of intensity. If you have any form of exercise, it can be a source of energy. Similarly, if you have some sort of artistic hobbies like painting or sculpting, you can channel that negative energy in the form of intense attention to detail.

Understand that the power of anger doesn't have to be all consuming and mentally cancerous. It can be redirected. It can be channeled. But it requires discipline.

Chapter 13: Choose to Read The Situation Under The Best Light

By this point, you are doing really well because you're defusing your anger. You've also managed to reduce the things that you can be angry about. At this level, you should have a fairly manageable level of raw emotions. It's not completely gone, but you're definitely well on your way. To hammer another nail into the coffin of your anger issues, you need to learn how to read the situation in the best light possible.

How You Choose to Read A Situation Means A Lot

What do I mean by reading a situation? I've already stepped you through the process of focusing on certain facts. I've already taught you that you should be clear on the emotions that you use to paint a scenario for yourself because you may be dwelling on certain details that may not be there.

Reading a situation simply means how do you view what's happening to you? Is it a learning opportunity? Is it some sort of teachable moment? Or is it some sort of injury that you have to deal with? Is it some sort of ongoing insult to who you are, what you're about and your character? Of course, if you choose to read the situation based on the latter way, this makes your anger worse.

Still, by positioning the situation in somewhat black or white terms, you highlight your choice. This really is the point of this exercise. You're reminding yourself that you have a choice. You're going to boil everything down into a black and white choice because it makes it easier to remember that this is a choice. It's much harder to choose when the choices have many different colors, shades, and hues. But when you boil down everything into black and white, you are drawn to the light. It stands out. It is the clear alternative.

The bad stuff, the wrong direction, and decision stands out as well. Focus on the fact that you can always choose. You're not a slave to your emotions. You don't have to automatically respond in the worst way possible. Now that you have these black and white alternatives in front of you, you need to take things to the next level.

Find the Best Light

Now that it's clear to you what kind of reactions are available and you have really boiled them down into a star choice, this should give you the motivation to look at the facts again. Revisit the facts and your interpretation of them. Is there any other way to analyze this? Is there another way to look at how is your experience in the situation and how it connects to many things happening in your life? Can you explain why you're tending to feel a certain way?

The more you do this, the more you learn about yourself. Maybe this person who said a weird joke triggered you so much not because the person is just some sort of scumbag who has it in for you, but maybe because you're frustrated in other areas of your life. If you see things in this light in how you connect core issues with what's happening in front of you, you gain perspective. You're less likely to go with your worst instincts.

Instead, you say to yourself, "Am I reacting this way because I'm frustrated and angry about other parts in my life? Maybe it's not this person or situation or that memory. Instead, it's something else. Maybe, if I took care of the big stuff going on in my life, I would be less angry. There would be fewer things to be upset about."

Focus on the experience and how it connects to other core issues happening in your life. You might be surprised at how you connect the dots.

Create A Positive Feedback Link

Now that you're seeing the situation in black and white terms and you have allowed yourself to check out the facts and your interpretation, the next step is to try to come up with a positive feedback. It's not always easy, but when you have a start choice in front of you, it definitely gives you the emotional urgency you need to do this. It takes work, but it can be done. The best part is the more you do this, the easier it will get over time. But you need to start.

How do you create a positive feedback link? First of all, by understanding that you are responding based on certain core issues in your life, you get perspective. You understand now why things are playing out the way they are. You also become aware of the fact that it doesn't have to lead to the worst-case scenario. It doesn't have to lead to you burning your bridges, hurting a lot of feelings or having stuff blow up in your face.

Look at the facts and see if there are anything that's neutral. Is there anything that's not as bad? Once you're able to do this, the next step is to create a positive feedback link. You start by focusing on that one time you handled your anger right. You may be thinking that you really are bad at this or your anger always gets the better of you. I know where you're coming from, but there should be at least one time where you were able to handle this raw emotion correctly. Can you remember that? Can you focus on that?

Now that you have that memory in your mind, ask yourself, "How did it feel when I was able to do that?" At the very least, you should feel some sort of relief. Pay attention to any other positive results that you have gotten by handling your anger right.

Once you are clear about these, feel good about those positive events. Always remember the emotions you felt. These are great emotions. You felt in control. You felt like you don't have to fall head over heels into anger, pain, and guilt.

Now that you are clear of those events, actively connect this to the anger you're feeling now. Again, for this to work, you have to do this over and over again. The good news is when we allow ourselves to think about certain memories, we do get triggered. Use that as practice.

Actively connect these past memories where you felt that you mastered your emotions and associate them with your anger. This way, when you feel anger, you're constantly reminded of that time or times or the past situations when you handled it in the best way possible. This way, your anger no longer pushes you to take these harsh steps. You don't have to say really hurtful stuff. You don't have to physically assault somebody, instead, your anger triggers past memories of you acting the right way.

If you follow all the steps above, this becomes easier to do because at this point, your viewing the situation in the best light possible. Now, don't get too optimistic. Sometimes, the best light possible is not much of an improvement. But when you create a positive feedback link, you are able to connect to a sense of control and willful action that reminds you that you can still choose regardless of how intense your emotions are right now.

Chapter 14: Focus on The Negative Consequences If You Constantly Act In Anger

I wish I could tell you that everyone is motivated by striving or gaining. These people are called proactive. They like something, they imagine it, they have hopes, wishes, and dreams. Accordingly, they make all sorts of plans to actively work on turning those dreams into reality. This is the ideal for most people that we should be proactive, we should be active.

Let me tell you the reality, most of us are reactive in nature. We're not motivated so much by our hopes, dreams and desire for gain. We can understand the power of ambition. We might think that it's a very good thing, but deep down inside, most people are motivated by fear. That's right. They only lift a finger to change their situation when they feel their backs are against the wall. They only make positive moves and changes when they are on the verge of losing something very precious to them.

You have to understand that as Anthony Robins says, people don't do the things they should, instead, they do things that they feel they must do. People who are reactive only take action when they feel that they must take action. Anything short of that, they stay in the same place. They're not happy by any stretch of the imagination, but they require a push.

Don't feel too bad if you are a reactive person. Most people are. Welcome to the club. If this is your mindset, then understand that there's really no right or wrong answer. You can be proactive or you can be reactive. It's okay. We're all oriented differently. What I want you to focus on is that you just need to ask yourself one key question so you can get the motivation you need as a reactive person to do the right thing with your anger. Ask yourself this question, "What do I stand to lose?" That's all you need to ask. That's a very powerful question for a reactive people because you are going to lose a lot.

Here is just a short list of what could happen if you blow it right now. If you act in the worst way possible out of anger, here are the things that could possibly happen. This is not theory. This is not just academic speculation. This is based on lived experience. This actually happens when people say really hurtful things or do stuff that ends in physical hurt or they end up in jail.

If you blow it, you end up hurting your relationships. You end up burning bridges. You end up destroying your reputation. You also could hurt your career. You can become an even worse hot head. This is actually one of the biggest dangers because if you give in to your worst instincts again and again and again, you feed your negative habits. They get stronger and stronger. It takes a lot more effort and it would take a lot more time to change them.

You also become a worse student. I'm not talking about being a student in any kind of academic setting, although that is definitely relevant. I'm talking about being a student of life. If you want to be successful in many areas of your life, you need to pick up certain lessons and we're always learning these lessons day to day. But if you are a very emotionally reactive and angry person, those lessons are just not going to sink in.

Finally, you stand to lose your health. I'm talking about not just your psychological and emotional health. I'm not just referring to your spiritual health. I'm also talking about your physical health. Research studies have indicated that prolonged high-stress levels lead to mental health issues, which leads to heart disease, blood pressure, cardiovascular problems and immune system degradation. Talk about bad news.

You lose all around. You burn your relationships, you burn your mental and emotional state, you screw up your ability to learn from life in general and just as bad, you physically mess up yourself. You lose a lot. I want you to focus on this. I want you to get pumped up about this. I want you to get scared of this. You have to look at this situation, not as something that can happen or may happen, instead, I want you to understand that if you don't change, this is what is going to happen. It's a prophecy. It's guaranteed. It may not be as extreme, but it's going to happen. And guess what? The damage is still the same.

Exaggerate the Threat of Loss

If you start having a tough time getting motivated by fear and the sense of potential loss, do this trick on yourself. Exaggerate the threat of loss in your mind. Instead of thinking of this as something that can happen, assume that it will. Assume that the next time you get angry or do something rash because of your raw emotions that somebody really important to you will leave. Imagine yourself losing a job because of this.

Whatever worst case scenario you may have in your mind, focus on it. Paint a vivid 3D image of it in your mind. Allow yourself to get emotionally caught up in the visualization of the worst-case scenario. I want you to really jump in with both feet because I would like you to use this simulated experience to trigger a higher sense of urgency. Keep repeating this mental linkage between your anger and the things that could go wrong. You should start to fear it. You should start to say to yourself, "Well, I'm forced to keep it together. I'm forced to use these mental centering techniques and I'm forced to focus on facts. Otherwise, the threat of loss is too great."

Whether you're motivated by love or fear, it doesn't matter. You end up in the same place. You need to make that decision to create a new default reaction to anger. This can take quite some time. It definitely will take a lot of effort, but it's definitely worth doing.

Chapter 15: The More You Practice, The Better You Get

You may be thinking to yourself that this is really hard stuff. I understand where you're coming from. You are, after all, reprogramming yourself. For so many years, certain stimuli triggered certain reactions from you. It happened day after day. Week after week. Month after month. Year after year. The more you repeat it, the stronger the links become. It's as if you're dealing with something that is just hardwired into your personality.

I've got some news for you. There's no need for you to beat yourself up with unrealistic expectations. Allow yourself to not expect overnight results. What's important here is to just constantly test these techniques. Constantly use them. Find yourself in certain situations where negative emotions are just right under the surface. Test them. If you don't find yourself in those situations, think about unpleasant memories that usually trigger you.

Whatever you need to do, constantly test these materials. The more you test, the better you get. Why? You learn how to fit these techniques to how you actually deal with things. Remember, everybody's different. We all come from different backgrounds or ways of life and we all have different experiences. These differences can add up to quite a bit.

You have to look at your set of circumstances and how you normally deal with things and plug in the information that I have taught you. This is only going to happen if you find yourself in a situation where you're going to have to use them. In other words, you're testing yourself. Constantly test yourself and you will get better at it.

To turbo-charge your results, you need to keep a journal. You're not just keeping mental bookmarks of where you are. You're not just making some sort of mental notation. Instead, you can see, based on certain stimuli, you will be able to see areas for improvement and most importantly, you will be able to understand that you're making progress. It's definitely easy to get pumped up when you see that you've gone a long way from where you started. That's good news. Allow yourself to be motivated by that good news.

Conclusion

Get started. Regardless of what you do, you need to get started. This doesn't mean you have to get started overnight. Don't do that. Instead, focus on getting started. Don't focus on whether that you'll get started when it feels right. Don't trick yourself into thinking that once everything else in your life falls into place then you will do this. That's not going to happen. Instead, you need to do this first so things will fall into place. This is foundational to you getting your act together at many different levels of your life. This should be the high priority.

Even worse, don't wait for other people to get their acts together. I hope you don't need me to remind you of how futile that could be because hey, let's face it. It's hard enough changing ourselves. Can you imagine changing other people? Instead, you should focus on yourself and pick a date. That's what you need to do.

Now that you've read this book, do you see that this can help you get out from under the severe strain and pressure of your anger issues? You need to pick a date. You have to pick a date that's not too soon and not too late.

The problem with picking a date that is too soon is that you end up freaking yourself out. When it comes, you're unable to step up. As I mentioned earlier, when you pick a date that is too late, don't be surprised if your life packs that time with other tasks and other issues.

You have to pick something that is imminent enough to get you pumped up, but not so soon that it freaks you out and paralyzes you. It shouldn't be too far off in the future that you feel that there's really no urgency.

Regardless of what you do, once you pick a date, don't give yourself an excuse not to start. You just have to do it again and again and again. Do it. Do it. Do it. Give yourself plenty of opportunities to practice the techniques mentioned in this book. Believe me, regardless of where you are or the time, you will have an opportunity. Why? Well, you might not be around stressful people. You might not be in a toxic situation currently, but you definitely have memories that trigger you. Start with those. There's really no excuse for you not to test yourself over and over again until you master everything that I've taught you in this book.

I wish you nothing but great success, peace, happiness, and love.

Access Your FREE Report

Thank you for downloading this book. As a way of showing my appreciation, I want to give you a **FREE REPORT** along with this book.

Free Report: 4 Amazing Techniques That Will Help You to Control Your Anger!

This Free Report will teach you about-

- 4 Techniques to Control Your Anger.
- Stop Being A Complainer: I'll Show How
- The Power of Forgiveness.
- Why You Should Practice Forgiveness.
- Avoid Anxiety & Stress using 5 Simple Tips.

Please visit the below link to access your Free Report!

http://geni.us/freeanger

55941045R00070

Made in the USA
Columbia, SC
18 April 2019